The Futurism of the Instant

The Futurism of the Instant

Stop-Eject

PAUL VIRILIO

Translated by Julie Rose

polity

First published in French as *Le Futurisme de l'instant* © Editions Galilée, 2009

This English edition © Polity Press, 2010
Reprinted 2011

This book is supported by the French Ministry of Foreign Affairs, as part of the Burgess programme run by the Cultural Department of the French Embassy in London (www.frenchbooknews.com)

Polity Press
65 Bridge Street
Cambridge CB2 1UR, UK

Polity Press
350 Main Street
Malden, MA 02148, USA

ISBN-13: 978-0-7456-4863-7
ISBN-13: 978-0-7456-4864-4(pb)

A catalogue record for this book is available from the British Library.

Typeset in 12 on 17 pt Garamond Light
by Servis Filmsetting Ltd, Stockport, Cheshire
Printed and bound in Great Britain by the MPG Books Group

The publisher has used its best endeavours to ensure that the URLs for external websites referred to in this book are correct and active at the time of going to press. However, the publisher has no responsibility for the websites and can make no guarantee that a site will remain live or that the content is or will remain appropriate.

Every effort has been made to trace all copyright holders, but if any have been inadvertently overlooked the publisher will be pleased to include any necessary credits in any subsequent reprint or edition.

For further information on Polity, visit our website: www.politybooks.com

Contents

Translator's Preface

How to catch the linguistic charge, all the subtle implications of the writer's lexicon and cultural reference, is the job of any translation. When it comes to the work of Virilio, where the polemics are inseparable from a poetics that is symphonic, with meanings and rhythms circling and swelling within each work and between all the works of the oeuvre as a whole, meeting the challenge of the job means doing justice to the almost abstract discursive rigour, without missing the irony or flattening the punning wit so crucial to the sense.

The Futurism of the Instant presents one specific challenge that seems to beg a note by way of explanation. Virilio's poetic and clever use of the verb *emporter* and its derivatives – *emport, emporté, emportable, emportement* – can't be precisely reproduced in English, at least, not by one word. We just don't have one word that does all the things *emporter* does, down through all the layers and registers of tone and reference. *Emporter* can, for example, mean to take or carry, in the sense of to remove, transport, take away; to carry or sweep away, or to get carried away, in a metaphorical or emotional sense; to take off (an arm), to blow away (a hat), and so on. It can mean to kill, to carry off and it can mean to win, to win out, prevail. The reflexive verb *s'emporter* means to fly into a rage. Food *à emporter* is takeaway, food to go. There is always a sense of movement – away – but the scope of that movement is very broad.

Virilio mobilizes many of these meanings throughout *The Futurism of the Instant*, building reverberations with each use, even in the most 'practical' application, which is the primary sense of *emporter* here: to carry away, to remove. Next in importance is the sense of carrying the day, triumphing.

The noun *emport*, used here in the aviation term, *capacité d'emport*, meaning 'maximum payload', has no other listed use. I've used 'carrying capacity' to broaden the scope of reference, while keeping the connection to *emporter* in its sense of to carry (away).

And in this spirit of acknowledging the clear, if rare, limitations imposed by linguistic difference, I've settled on 'portable' as the least unsatisfactory approximation for *emport* in the phrase *révolution de l'emport* and so on, with occasional references to removability and exportability, as the context required. I've kept the French to flag such instances.

In an essay with the sweeping themes of mass population flows, displacement, exodus, exile, expatriation, exurbanism, extraplanetary exploration, any congestion in the clean flow of Virilio's prose must be slated to the translator.

JR

1 Stop-Eject

Far from here – that's my aim.

Franz Kafka

According to a report published in 2007 by the British non-governmental organization, Christian Aid, the number of future environmental migrants is estimated at close to one billion. This document makes the claim that 645 million people will be displaced from their homes over the next forty years because of large-scale development projects like intensive mining activity or the building of hydroelectric dams. Of these, 250 million will be displaced by phenomena related to climate change, floods and submersion of coastal land and, ultimately, at least 50 million people will be displaced by conflicts produced by such catastrophic upheavals

1

entailing the demographic resettlement of the planet.

Faced with this unprecedented migration crisis, which is incomparably more serious than the immigration of the industrial age, and which is already being called the migration offensive of the third millennium, the issue of urbanization in the contemporary world might be seen in terms that undermine the customary distinction between sedentariness and nomadism.

In fact, after the pluralist era of *sustainable staying-put* in the different neighbourhoods of registered urban land – a form of *stationary* settlement that once, in antiquity, introduced the notion of 'citizenship', as deriving from political localization, and with it, ultimately, of the 'legally constituted state' of nations – the era of *habitable circulation* is now dawning with the transpolitical delocalization that is now overturning the geopolitics of settlement in the age of globalization. And this is happening at the precise moment that the teletechnologies of information are ensuring that sedentary man is at home everywhere, and the nomad nowhere, beyond the provisional accommodation offered by a now pointless trans-humance. That transhumance is now taking place, not only from one country to another. Now people are displaced within their very homeland from their heartland to some vague territory where refugee camps have not only taken over from the shanty towns of days gone by, but from the towns. The megalopolis of the excluded of all stripes, pouring in from all sides, has now come to rival the all-too-real megalopolis of the included, the ultracity.

The exoticism of misery thereby meets the exoticism of happy tourism, and it's not hard to imagine the scale of such a telescoping of these groups of people who have come adrift from their moorings in urbanity, as they did once, not so long ago, from their customary moorings in rurality. It's not hard to imagine, either, the scale of any traffic accident now that the traffic is no longer local, as it was in the days of the great invasions, but global.

Allowed to travel since 1997, 37 million Chinese

left their homeland last year. After the 2008 Olympic Games, you can bet that as many as 70 million will turn into tourists.

Note on that score that there has long been a floating population of close to 100 million destitute peasants in China, wandering around looking for work and most often winding up in the country's vast railway stations, as Chen Guidi and Wu Chuntao indicate: 'Peasants were kept out of the towns at the end of the 1950s by means of the grain distribution scheme and Mao Zedong's institution of an urban resident's permit – the *hukow* – which divided society into two classes: urban and rural. … From that point on, town and country would be like two vehicles travelling on different tracks.'[1]

After the 'sustainable' settlement that character-ized the population flows of past history, 'habit-able' circulation opens up dizzying perspectives for planetary resettlement.

---

[1] Chen Guidi and Wu Chuntao, *Will the Boat Sink the Water? The Life of China's Peasants*. New York: Public Affairs, 2006, tr. Zhu Hong, pp. 176–7.

4

Having first lost its suburbs and then its rural hinterland, the metacity of tomorrow won't long be able to resist the demographic pressure coming from its outland, which will drive the exodus of settlers without hope of returning to the sedentariness of the semi-autonomous city of our origins.

It's hard, in fact, to imagine the radiant future of 'sustainable development' in the face of the hullabaloo over communications and telecommunications tools that are undeniably progressive, but also completely incapable of dealing with the transpolitical tragedy of ecology. These tools can no more deal with the greenhouse gas effect on the *atmosphere* than with the effect on the *dromosphere* of the mass exodus of out-of-work hordes.

Forget the instant city that the English futurists imagined. What developers now have in mind is a non-stop circus, a long-haul cruise for the exiles of outsourcing. This is the 'war of each against all', the ultimate figure of a sort of civil war of movement that will take over from the ancestral siege war of the commune or of the underprivileged suburban outskirts.

Actually, what we are now seeing, as the third millennium gets under way, is the emergence of an absolutely unknown form of ex-territori-alization of human potential that is soon likely to rule out all possibility of any kind of urban potential. This will lead to a new form of eccen-tricity, whereby the quest for an exoplanet, an ultraworld, as a replacement for the old one, now too polluted, will double up, here below, with the quest for an ultracity, a sort of logisti-cal platform – something which the airport, the port and the railway station have only ever been scaled-down models of.

Skipping the right to citizenship by virtue of birth in a country defined by geopolitics and the historical persistence of sites, the *révolution de l'emport*, or portable revolution, will round off the transport revolution, and the revolution in transmission will land us in this interactive planisphere that will, they say, be capable of sup-plementing the overly cramped biosphere and its five continents. It will do this thanks to the feats in information technology of a virtual continent, the great colony of cyberspace taking over from the empires of yore.

Emergency exit: If the major event for anthropologists of the moment is demographic growth over the past century or so – from one and a half billion individuals in 1900 to six billion in the year 2000 – when this is coupled with the boom in instantaneous transmission and supersonic transport, the result will be one billion displaced persons tomorrow, deportees everywhere you look. We'll need to somehow rehouse these people and we'll need to do so in less than half a century. That seems quite simply impossible to achieve, unless we abandon the city, the semi-autonomous town, and go back to camps, and the precariousness of 'tent cities'.

In 1900, rural exodus was in full swing in the West and one in ten of the planet's inhabitants was a city dweller. Today, it's one in two; in other words, four times the 1950 number. That means there are three billion sedentary metropolitans – at the very moment that urban exodus is just getting started with the prospect of those one billion dispossessed refugees by the year 2050 . . .

After the general mobilization of the Great War, which was a direct result of the ideology of the 'people in arms', and the total mobilization of the Second World War, what is being fore-shadowed in this great economic and ecological transhumance is not so much the final struggle as the integral mobilization of populations driven from their native land and from geolocalization. This was before the latter mutated into a mere matter of satellite positioning (GPS or Galileo), and when it was still the most important politi-cal fact in the history of humanity, whereby the *hic et nunc* and geopolitics were tied in together with the City of our origins, the *polis* with its 'right to citizenship based on birth in a country' as opposed to the 'right of citizenship based on kinship' upheld by nomadic tribes. All this just to give shape to the place (lieu) of the social bond (lien) and of a 'common right' that used to be expressed perfectly well, as it happens, by the

axis mundi of the cities of antiquity which repre-
sented *the centre of the world*.

But let's get back to the sudden downward
drift set off by a depopulation process through
which exurbanism is gearing up to supplant the
suburbanism of the outskirts of the industrial era.
At the end of 2007, the cities of The Hague and
Rotterdam alone were facing an influx of 40,000
new migrants. The idea of setting up containers to
accommodate Polish labourers was being touted
… And nobody was put off by such a blatantly
segregationist practice at local government level
in relation to *foreigners* from the Eastern European
Community. In Amsterdam, for instance, the now
famous containers in the port where dockers once
used to get together today house Dutch students;
and Algeco, the maker and operator of on-site
sheds which recently bought out its American
subsidiary, Williams Scotsman, has become the
world leader in modular space solutions.

We might note in passing that, now that the
great race to speed up progress has been won
once and for all by instantaneous transmission

equipment, all that transport equipment has to offer is the slight advantage of a growing and still indispensable *capacité d'emport*, maximum payload or carrying capacity. Yet the constraints due to dwindling oil supplies and growing pollution will shortly necessitate restrictions on movement and an exponential growth in quantities carried since the logics or, more exactly, the logistics, of a 'just-in-time and stockless' distribution system now entail gigantism in loads to the detriment of the old warehouses – whence the endlessly increasing importance of the intermodal platform in freight transportation. Today intermodal platforms ensure transit and break of load (transshipment) between one means of transport and another, whether land, sea or air. They do this for the 'bulk carriers', the vast container ships, that serve the different quarters of the ultracity under construction, this 'capital to end all capitals' thrown up by international economic integration.

So it is well and truly under way, this sort of post-urban revolution that will drive the twenty-first century. It's a portable revolution, a *révolution de l'emport*, with consequences for the history of planning and development that could prove singularly more devastating than last century's revolution in industrial transport. This is why, right now, the rug is being pulled out from under sedentary settlement of an urban species which is, in the end, as threatened as the rural species was up until the revelation of food insecurity that has now hit us, with the totally symptomatic business of cereal-based biofuels.

As Heidemarie Wieczorek, the German Minister for Economic Cooperation and Development, put it: 'The right to food takes precedence over the right to mobility.' In fact, the sudden emergence of the ultracity is incomparably more frightening in its socio-political implications than is the contemporary urban sprawl triggered by the rise of the domestic automobile.

With exurbia gearing up to outpace good old suburbia and its tentacular conurbations, we hardly bat an eyelid any more over the emphasis firms now place on outsourcing production – including research and development – to the detriment of their former localization within a historic space that is our cultural heritage. And so, for some little time now, the external has been winning hands down over the internal every-where you turn, and geophysical history has been turned inside out like a glove!

Hence the successive generations of 'portable' objects, whereas objects were once happy to be 'fixed' and precisely situated. Hence also, as I've pointed out before, the radical reversal of the relationship between nomadism and seden-tariness that is at the origins of settlement. Now accompanying baggage far outweighs vehicles of all kinds in importance, with computers, mobile phones, electronic transponder bracelets and the GPS, the watch that now tells the place the way the old one told the time. These devices anticipate the implants of the transplantation age such as the Radio Frequency Identification tag, a microchip GPS tracking implant. As we all know: every time the speed of movement increases, monitoring and traceability increase in step.

A bit further down the track and identity

will give way to the traceability of the private citizen, of any distinct person – as the CNIL, the *Commission nationale informatique et liberté*, already fears is happening.

Just like the elementary particle at the heart of Geneva's Great Accelerator – the Large Hadron Collider – we will then not only be 'filed', but tracked, making knowing where we permanently reside completely pointless.

'The automobile has turned us into homeless vagrants', Adorno remarked, incredulous, some little time ago … What can we say, today, in the age of general '*emportement*', the culture of root-less rage, that is now taking over from the political *commitment* of the past century, except that the 'escape velocity' generated by technical progress turns us into deportees of a new kind. And that this leads directly, not to the extermination of genocide, but to the geocide of the externaliza-tion – outsourcing – of 'urbankind' and, soon, of humankind in general. The pathological sequelae of this are unknown … The myth of some happy, beneficial neo-nomadism won't long survive the experience of being locked down in a closed circuit, within the now relative non-expanse of this life-bearing star of ours.

A veritable astronomical revolution in the continuum of history, the globalization of post-industrial interactivity literally turns the complex orientation of human activity on its head. Hence the abuse of the terms 'deregulation' and 'relocation'. Hence also the repeat divorces afflicting the urbankind of our once 'civilized' societies, as well as the whole array of foreign policies, now discredited in the name of an eccentric planetary globalization. The whole process is aided and abetted, we might note in passing, by certain astrophysicists who hide behind a feigned concern about pollution of the earthly environment in a desperate bid to discover, somewhere in the universe, a Super Earth, capable, in its gigantic dimensions, of providing a positive answer to Mother Earth's negative ecological footprint due to the damage done by progress, our tiny little telluric planet finally proving insalubrious and unfit for life.

We must point out here that this quest for an

exoplanet entails a quest for an ultraworld to come, which will suddenly loom up like a cosmic model of the ultracity, thereby reversing the very notion of symbolic centrality, along with the sedentariness of the geopolitical *hic et nunc*. For if the Axis of the World ran through the heart of the city of antiquity long ago, tomorrow's ultracity, the Metacity, will be outsourced to the middle of nowhere!

Deportation yesterday, delocalization, exclusion today – these are all terms for a semantic slide that signals, if not exodus, then at least forced exile. They are the expression of a truly 'repulsive' globalization that no one can now contest, as though last century's mass tourism had only been an early warning sign of the dispossession to come, a sort of warm-up, getting the hordes ready for the ordeal of an off-piste trip, with leisurely wayfaring far from home turf foreshadowing the take-off out of this world offered by space tourism, with a view to one day securing the public salvation of humanity!

15

And so, following last century's destruction and its mass extermination, the Time, 'real time', seems to have come for social deconstruction and its frantic externalization, or outsourcing.

'Going and seeing elsewhere', and 'seeing it coming' right here – this alternating movement seems to endlessly accelerate, oscillating between the exotic impulse to get up and go and the expulsion of those excluded from an international integration that is now terminal and not inaugural, as it once was at, say, the time of the discovery of the Americas.

In fact, geophysical space is no longer an adjustment variable for the economy of our travels, as it was in the era of past globalizations.

Here again, the reversal is evident, since the much-touted 'End of History' is scarcely more than an optical (dromoscopic) illusion that mainly masks the end of geography and its continuum. The *révolution de l'emport massif*, or bulk portable revolution, is only the ultimate consequence of the *emportement*, the getting carried away, involved in accelerating reality, and of the exhaustion of the resources produced by the geo-diversity of a globe that can't go on much longer sustaining the exhaustion of long distances.

If you listen to the travel agents, our contemporaries can't possibly be considered 'catastrophists' since 'tour operators are booked out'. . . Certainly, today's tourists aren't pessimists in the manner of the well-heeled voyagers of bygone days who travelled for pleasure. It's worse. What they're beginning to feel is good old-fashioned cabin fever, the claustrophobia experienced by those buried alive by their own 'carbon footprint'!

They say that voluntary guinea pigs are already training to survive the long voyage to the planet Mars, vicariously, in an airtight compartment onboard a container designed to familiarize them with the gruelling expulsion of a long-haul exile that could well turn out to be one-way.

Actually, the current academic quarrel among astrophysicists over the comparative advantages of robotic probes of the 'Mars Express' type, as opposed to manned flights, illustrates rather well how powerfully motivated are the apostles of the *révolution de l'emport*, a portable revolution exporting to the ultraworld. Which might explain the dubious appeal of the 'lunar module', that container that can do anything, but is especially good at undoing statics, the stability of being rooted in one's native soil, and promoting instead the eccentricity of a non-stop trip.

Didn't we see an apple-green container only a little while ago, in Paris? It sat on the terrace of the Musée d'art contemporain at the top of the Palais de Tokyo, opposite the Musée des arts premiers. Put there by the Hilton Group, it was designed to be rented out as night-time accommodation.

Similarly, following the capsule hotel, designed by Japanese architect Kisho Kurokawa, Gatwick airport and then Heathrow airport, both close to London, now offer their 'Yotel' clientele cylindrical cabins eight square metres in size, plonked on the ground inside the terminal buildings for the benefit of (supernumerary) transit passengers.

Note that once again, it's not just the performance of the Stock Exchange that suddenly gets disconnected from the real economy. Now robbed of any connection to fiduciary experience or to the nature of a housing stock that is clearly in crisis, it's actually the whole of the political economy of nations that is suffering today from the excesses of a catastrophic race for instant profit. They say we need to relativize any approach to, or 'geopolitical' analysis of, this situation, so as to free ourselves from locality and even, in the near future, as we've seen, from the incredibly constricting overall territory of the earthly star.

With this in mind, we can get a better measure of the relationships of cause and effect at play in the bulk exile of populations, starting with the most vulnerable, but ending, soon, we anticipate, in the headlong rush of the well-heeled, whose ambulatory madness as tourists is never more than a clinical symptom of loss of bearings or sudden disorientation. The subprime mortgage crisis in the United States illustrates to perfection the crisis in the construction and public works industries, with firms involved anticipating disaster in the stability of real estate, right here and now, by diversifying their activities and opting into so-called 'booming sectors' such as motor-way franchises, media and energy outlets and, of course, high-flow industrial-scale port facilities whose infrastructure will very soon be swamped by the requirements of the high-volume traffic and gigantic 'load transfers' involved, container carriers and other methane-fuelled tankers never ceasing to swell, to grow in obesity…

Just-in-time and stockless, that adage of inter-continental traffic, undermines the places where break of load between transport and *l'emport*, the exportable cargo carried, occurs. After the trans-formation of dockyards into industrial wasteland – in Liverpool, London, Hamburg, Amsterdam – it's no longer the architecture of the warehouse that is feeling the impact of the bulk carriers and their logistics. It's now the urbanism of cities on the horizontal coastline of loading and unload-ing zones, as well as of airport hubs on a vertical coastline. This is to say nothing more of railway stations, which have gradually turned into transit megalopolises, terminals ultimately ungovernable, as we see in Paris, Berlin, Moscow.

'I've never had an objective. I'm a path, not a goal.' So said Daniel Libeskind, the man responsible for the redevelopment of the 'Ground Zero' site in New York, not long ago.

Coming from an architect, that is a real revelation of the decline of statics, of material resistance and the fixity of real estate that not so long ago characterized the persistence of the city.

So, the adage of the builders of the city of antiquity – Plot. Divide Into Lots. Build – needs to be replaced by Plot. Divide Into Lots. Get Out, now that the vanishing line of the trajectory is supplanting the fixed point and the objective axiality of the city.

And so, the upgrade of the Saint-Charles neighbourhood in Marseilles prompts the operations manager for the new unit, which now links the railway and bus stations, to say: 'The historic notion of a station is old-hat. Saint-Charles Station must, of course, remain a transport centre, but it must eventually become a town centre.' Once again, the die is cast. The centre of the ultracity is called on to supplant the age-old town centre, tomorrow, and to do so within a 'just-in-time' dynamic which, after the rural exodus of the nineteenth and twentieth centuries, will lead to an urban exodus destined, in the twenty-first century, to achieve the exurbanism of resettlement of the world.

'Without a doubt, the United States has entered a new era in transportation,' the US Secretary of Transportation, Norman Mineta, declared in 2002, at a conference on homeland security, referring to 'an era where a cunning and remorseless enemy can challenge one of America's most cherished freedoms: freedom of movement'.

Despite the deceptive appearances of international terrorism in the year 2001, but also of the terrorism directed at Atocha railway station in Madrid in 2004, the enemy is first and foremost the sphere of accelerating reality, this prospective dromosphere that will be able to do away with expanse, tomorrow, in the very latest of historic globalizations. This explains the cabin fever presented by a humanity now deprived of a future and instead faced with the foreclosure of the space-time of the common world, in a lockdown that is both carceral and panoptic, in which the globalitarianism of Progress will come to mean control of movement, of travel flows.

In what would be the antithesis of the 'radiant future' touted by the totalitarianisms of yore, the mobile home and the 'non-stop tour' will take over from the semi-autonomous city and the claustropolis will dominate the ancient cosmopolis everywhere you turn.

And so, after the twentieth century's Futurism of long-term History, denounced by Daniel Lévy and celebrated by Marinetti, the time will then have come for this futurism of the instant, which Octavio Paz spoke to us about, observing bitterly: 'The moment is uninhabitable, just like the future.'

It is this form of insalubrious uninhabiting that today speaks to us through the exoduses, through the distant exiles, through all this dislocation of expatriation that is only ever deportation in disguise – not, as in days gone by, propelling people towards the extermination of the camps, towards genocide, any more, but driving them towards the externalization, the outsourcing, of the ultracity to come, the genocide of the twilight of places, the exhaustion of the resources produced by the geodiversity of the terrestrial globe.

'We are all at the bottom of a hell where every moment is a miracle,'[2] Cioran noted, thereby describing what was then the very latest of futurisms: the futurism of acceleration of reality in the twentieth century.

Here we touch on the now critical question of the *political economy of speed* – or, rather, its denial – posed by the experts of a macrofinancial system where the political economy of wealth and its associated speculation has been transferred to software packages, mathematical automatons. For this software, space is absolutely not an adjustment variable any more, since they only work through the 'miracle' of the futurism of

---

[2] Emil Cioran, *The New Gods.* New York: Quadrangle, 1974, tr. Richard Howard.

the instant – in other words, a 'transfer accident', the imposture of immediacy, which excludes all expanse just as it does all true duration and, with it, the rational intelligence guiding the geopolitics of nations.

Speaking of this 'hell', at the bottom of which we all repose thanks to the feats of the demiurges of the world economy, let's hear what a judge handling illegal immigration cases in Europe has to say: 'We're in danger of shortly being dragged into a diabolical cycle. It sends shivers down your spine when you learn, for example, that some migrants mutilate their fingers to avoid having their fingerprints taken and identified.'

When you know that around 20 million people apply for entry to the Schengen area every year, you get a pretty good idea of the growing size of the massive flows of people who will soon be set adrift from their social moorings as well as their specifically territorial ties. You also get a pretty good idea of the growing importance of a sort of 'large-scale battue', a hunt for civilians, extending the rural exodus of the final years of the second millennium into the third, and, especially, those long convoys travelling east in the mass deportation of populations that preceded their pure and simple extermination. For the new 'war on civilians' is no longer content just to use railways and the marshalling yards they come with. It now adds charter flights to these, in a bid to enforce a mass depopulation brought on by the evil spells, economic as well as ecological, of an unbearable Progress.

That's the reason for the draconian border controls put in place by customs officers and border patrols, with the biometric passport supplanting the old identity card, and itself soon to be supplanted by the credit card, as though purchasing power had once and for all taken over from 'staying power', the power to dwell somewhere together …

In fact, the lack of delay, the lack of any interval of time, that now characterizes macro-economic systems in the era of interactive globalization, doesn't so much ratchet up competition between nations, as the World Trade Organization would have us believe. It tends more to induce the opening of hostilities between civilian populations now threatened on all sides in confrontations in which resettlement of the terrestrial globe is now such an urgent issue that soon no metropolitan geopolitics will be able to deal with it.

To try, as they are doing, to go beyond the sovereignty of nations in favour of 'sovereign wealth funds' would clearly mean before long destroying the *domiciliary inertia*, the 'staying-put', that we have known throughout History, thereby triggering a fatal process of deconstruction – deconstruction of the city and of a 'metropolitics' that stood surety for a specifically territorial legitimate state. All this, in aid of a few branch sites, like the ones being trialled in the 'artificial earthly paradises' and condominiums that are dotted around here and there, today, with the insularity of urban land making way for archipelagos of private islands, such as those in Dubai and elsewhere. But these won't hold out, any longer than the 'resettlement camps', against the tsunami of the panic-stricken hordes to be resettled, this human tidal wave of close to a billion exiles that no one will be able to decently house in under half a century.

So, let's not be under any illusions! What is happening in Africa and Asia, with the 50 million people qualified by the Office of the United Nations High Commissioner for Refugees as 'victims of forced displacement', is no more than a clinical symptom of the *domiciliary emancipation*, the freeing up of settled living currently under way that will in turn hit Europe and the Americas and the rest of the developed world. As one French author writes, 'There is no outside, no physical space between the global and the sum of all nation states.'[3] And the so-called 'transit towns' of refugee camps will never make authentic cities, no matter what their demography, any more than the shanty towns made true suburbs.

Here, a revealing figure is called for: during the

---

[3] Michel Agier, *On the Margins of the World: The Refugee Experience Today.* Cambridge, UK and Malden, MA: Polity 2008, tr. David Fernbach, p. 40 (translation modified).

First World War, mobilization set some 65 million men in motion. Well, currently, the number is practically the same, since that figure of 50 million clearly doesn't include the invisible mass of illegal immigrants, who are the missing energy of the expanding world of populations in exile.

General mobilization in the twentieth century, global mobilization on the cusp of the twenty-first … Following the siege war of the Paris Commune in the nineteenth century, the war of movement of civilians has just broken out. It is a war that dissolves the notions of centre and periphery in these days of massive depopulation, when economic rationales to do with 'purchasing power' or 'staying power' have become interchangeable in the exclusion of a world where the workforce has, it would seem, lost its civilizing value in favour of the madness of electronic automation of production.

What is shaping up here, in this universe that's so much busier excluding than expanding, is no longer, no matter what they say, the return of the cosmopolis, or even of the claustropolis of gated communities or high-rise towers. What is shaping up, above all, is the marshalling yard, that 'terminus of last wishes' that Cendrars talked about in *Trans-Siberian Prose*.

This is the revelation of a fundamentally transpolitical ultracity, where the habitable staying-put of bygone days has abandoned the public square to the parking lot, and to the uninhabitable circulation of each against all; a universal civil war in which the trajectography of real-time exchanges has supplanted the place (lieu) of the social bond (lien) of domiciliation.

On this score, we might read Emmanuel Levinas: 'This world in which reason becomes more and more self-conscious is not habitable. It is hard and cold, like those warehouses where goods that can't satisfy pile up; impersonal like factory hangars where manufactured things remain abstract, true in terms of quantifiable truths and swept away into the anonymous circuit of the economy.'[4]

---

[4] Emmanuel Levinas, *Difficult Freedom: Essays on Judaism*, tr. Seán Hand. Baltimore: Athlone Press, 1990, p.32 (translation modified).

That's it, all right, this 'digital disruption' in which the reign of quantity is mobilized to sweep away everything in its path, in the name of immediate profit, that veritable geocruiser of an astronomical financial history, in which the just-in-time delivery systems of the closed circuit of the world economy turn the warehouse, or the abandoned dock, into the latest vehicle in a 'mass movement' of Progress that destroys, one by one, the statics of common places, along with the stability of social bonds.

This is the futurism of an uninhabitable instant, just as Octavio Paz sensed was coming, chiming with Emmanuel Levinas's philosophy. It is a pro-gressivism in which it is no longer a matter of leaving in order to get there safe and sound any more so much as of getting out in order to clear the terrain for a future 'twilight of places'. For want of actual borders between states, the terrain now offers nothing more than the catastrophe of continental entry-points for the greater profit of people smugglers pouring in from everywhere.

2 The Ultracity

It's really amazing, when you think about it, that we've got to the point where we consider a *levée en masse* or 'general mobilization' perfectly natural and where the idea of an armed nation goes without saying. You could see this as being due to force of numbers alone: 'Putting huge masses of combatants in motion is in line with the quantitative nature of modern civilization,'[1] as René Guénon signalled a while back already, heralding the 'Reign of Quantity' that would later lead to the *révolution de l'emport massif*, the bulk carrier revolution, that we are seeing today, with the energy crisis and the exhaustion of stocks of all

[1] René Guénon, *The Crisis of the Modern World*. New York: Sophia Perennis, 2004, tr. Arthur Osborne, Marco Pallis, and Richard C. Nicholson, p. 89.

kinds exposed by ecology, along with the immi-nent mutation of these 'just-in-time' distribution systems that were supposed to achieve the instant globalization of profit.

Here again, coming after the siege war of the city, the war of movement would later lead to the lightning war – blitzkrieg. This was delivered via the automobility of tank units, confirming what René Guénon had to say about the capacity of the 'transport revolution' to put the mass of civil-ian populations in motion – through exodus, exile, then deportation – thereby clearly flagging the scale of a sphere of accelerating history that claimed to be freeing us from the tyranny of dis-tance thanks to the auto-mobilization of a domes-tic individuality, and to be doing so without recourse to some order to leave for the front, or to any other kind of mobilization initiated by some Army ministry.

'The motor is knocking our doctrines around, just as it's playing havoc with our fortifications,' observed that tank soldier, Charles de Gaulle – the same man who, after he came to power, was to write in his *Memoirs*: 'Greatness has a firmer footing in distance than in turmoil.'

'Lightning war' of 1940, *lightning shutdown* – in a flash! – of the Hiroshima bomb of 1945: the propagation speed of the energy disaster went and crashed into the time barrier, ahead of the light barrier and the inauguration, in 2008, not of a new particle accelerator but of a great closed-circuit *collider*. Some people call this latter 'the cathedral', since the 27 kilometres of the Geneva speed ring are designed to reveal the hadron, a subatomic particle that certain scientists have named 'the God particle'.

'Energy is eternal delight,' thought William Blake, in his day. But what about its sources? The springs of energy certainly are no delight, as we've just noted, taking our cue from the Rimbaud of *Illuminations*, who wrote: 'How far away are the birds and the springs! This can only be the end of the world moving ahead.'

We had confirmation of the exhaustion of stocks during the last American presidential election campaign when the two candidates confronted each other over the issue of energy and the need 'to give, or not to give, Americans access to American oil'. In other words, whether to drill for oil on the continental shelf or to dig an offshore mine. The Republican candidate, John McCain, who made the energy independence of the United States the cornerstone of his campaign, went so far as to declare: 'We need to drill *here* and we need to drill *now*.'

Barack Obama, his Democrat adversary, remained opposed to drilling on the continental shelf of North America, but did accept offshore drilling and even – the ultimate crime for the superpower – to siphon off some seventy million barrels from the strategic reserve to bring down the price of oil. To which the Republican candidate's retort was, 'The strategic reserve of the United States exists for the needs of national security, not for those of the election of Barack Obama.'

In 1977, I wrote that speed is the world's old age. Thirty years later, the evidence of this is clear, since the impact of global mobilization has torpedoed the political economy of the wealth of nations that, until now, turned its back on a principle of acceleration that would no less undermine the history of a technical progress incompatible with the quantitative reserve necessary to the survival of nations.

And so, *ex abrupto*, the celebrated adage of just-in-time commercial distribution takes on quite a different meaning from that of 'just-in-time and at the fairest price' for a delirious 'single market'!

This is the degree zero of an economic script in which accumulation of wealth meant overlooking the ravages caused by the speed of acceleration of movement which leads to the chaos of a *systemic crisis*, such as the one we have been going through for a year at least now, in anticipation of the further undermining of all national and territorial identity. What will be promoted instead is the traceability of individuals and the chaos of the mass resettlement involved in exodus for societies that will once again be dispersed in diasporas. The original town is giving way to the *ultracity* produced by an exurbanism that is not so much metropolitan as omnipolitan, and this anticipates the not far-off colonial exodus to the *ultraworld* of a distant planet, some super-Earth likely to see the 'ecological footprint' of an unnatural progress grow to twice or three times its current size in an all-out exploitation of the reserves of the exoplanet in question.

In the face of such an unsatisfactory situation, we have no choice but to acknowledge that, from now on, the *capacité d'emport*, or maximum carrying capacity, outclasses the capacity of transport, no matter what its velocity.

So the future looks like belonging to 'bulk carriers' capable of containing, not only life and its products, but *extremophile survival*, as it's known by the exobiologists, those adepts at weightlessness for whom the vehicle is everything and the goal of the voyage of no value. Petrarch's saying about seafaring puts it so well: 'Navigating is vital, living is not.'

Nautical, aeronautical and shortly astronautical 'bulk carrier' – or Very High Building? That static vehicle of cooped-up 'above-ground' elevation is also, and every bit as much, a carrier, a *surrogate mother* for others, in a 'procreative tourism' that is getting bigger all the time in exotic locations. … These are all so many panicky signs of the imminent *révolution de l'emport*, carrying us away in bulk, which will have been brought on by the sudden revelation of the exhaustion of the resources the poet of *Illuminations* told us about, in days long gone.

According to Adorno, the automobile was going to turn us into homeless vagrants. In the United States, since the subprime crisis of 2007, that's a done deal; it's now the automobile industry that is bearing the brunt of the storm. But tomorrow, with the technologies of the *Emportable*, the Removable, what will remain of a person's homeland, of a precisely located identity that will soon be replaced by never-ending traceability on the part of sensors?

Ecology and nomadism have recently joined forces, what's more, in updating the old foolproof method of wartime regiments for exploiting the energy potential of the human body in motion.

Why not, for instance, recuperate the heat generated by crowds in transit to heat up public places? Why not capture the energy produced by motion and use it to make electricity for street lighting? It is still within the context of general mobilization that the United States' Defense Advanced Research Projects Agency (DARPA) is interested in these futurist projects.

We might hark back here to the rhythmical motion of troops that would soon be sent into combat in the trenches of the 'Great War', a war in which the generals calculated the victory of an advance by the number of its victims – the *renewable energy* of the bodies of infantrymen being equivalent to a mine ripe for all-out exploitation, with 'procreative' leave being designed for the replenishment of livestock for the conflicts of the future.

In the twenty-first century, the general staff of the great powers find that the soldier of the zero-death war ought to be equipped not only with a bullet-proof vest, but also with flexible armour, endowed with sensors and emitters capable of recuperating all the energies of the human body – in other words of increasing the *capacité d'emport*, the carrying capacity, of the warrior of the future, thanks to the 'technological obesity' of his various instruments.

After the 40-kilo backpack that the infantry-man of yore hauled around, the future looks like belonging to the development of *ergonomic instrumentation* of combat gear.

After the electronic handcuffs worn by delin-quents who are half-free and the GPS for all, it will be a matter, in sum, of converting the dynamism of crowds in motion and of animals in locomo-tion into recoupable energy. In this productivist perspective, the motto of the Olympic Games – Citius–Altius–Fortius, or faster, higher, stronger – would take on a quite different meaning from the one that applies to the performance of top-tier athletes, and the issue of doping in sport would then become a problem of pure metabolic productivity.

A researcher with the CNRS, the Centre national
de recherche scientifique, has spelled this out
clearly: 'Poor, low-frequency energy is, alas, the
double handicap of human movement',[2] thereby
giving us to understand that it would be appropriate in future to improve output by exploiting the
energy source of galloping population growth.
Which helps explain the choice of Beijing for the
last Olympic Games!

After the industrialization of death on the bat-
tlefields of the twentieth century, then in the
camps, the temptation is obviously great today
to *industrialize life*, life's 'extremophile' biology,
in the name of some vital productivity whereby
the exhaustion of fossil energies will force us
to exploit the *renewable energy* of a human
race undergoing accelerated population growth,
but whose 'energy handicap' will have to be
eliminated to best ensure environmental security.

In the wake of the evident excesses in consumption over the course of the past century, of

[2] *La Croix*, 8 August 2008.

which the *general mobilization* of nations was the early warning symptom, and in light of the current *global mobilization* of populations in transit which is its catastrophic extension, we now note that the relaunch of nuclear energy is not even seen as paradoxical, despite the warnings of people like Ulrich Beck, who recently wrote: 'The "existential concern" being awakened across the world by global risks has led to a contest to suppress large-scale risks in political discussion. The incalculable dangers to which climate change is giving rise are supposed to be "combated" with the incalculable dangers associated with nuclear power plants.'

Beck concludes: 'The actors who are supposed to be the guarantors of security and rationality – the state, science and industry – are engaged in a highly ambivalent game ... For they are urging the population to climb into an aircraft for which a landing strip has not yet been built.'[3]

There's that fabled notion of 'carrying capa-

---

[3] *Le Monde*, 7 August 2008.

city', *capacité d'emport*, again – only, this time, it's a matter of carrying the support of the hordes, thanks to the *lying by deterrence* that has only just replaced the *lying by omission* of an era in which freedom of expression didn't really exist after all.

'Nothing in the Universe is fixed,' noted Albert Einstein last century – that strange era in which Einstein was to reject the absolute values of space and time and recognize, in matter, an energy as it were solidified.

In the twenty-first century, it would certainly seem that this 'relativist' transmutation asks only to be applied to the mass of humanity as living matter.

Actually, after the territorial body of a minuscule planet, it is now the social body as a whole, as well as the animal body of each of its members, that the release of constituted, if not solidified, energies aspires to be applied to. The ecological revelation of the geophysical finiteness of our life-giving star leads, here below, to the revolutionary aspirations of a propaganda for

Progress that is less postmodern than, frankly, *post-historic*!

In fact, as has been clear since the eighteenth century, war has become the great test of History. Through its constant 'progress' and thanks to the militarization of science, war has been extended to nature, to nature's geophysical dimension. So much so, that it has become this unnatural dimension that endlessly shatters the positivity of the experimental findings of science – or, rather, of an operative, instrumental technoscience, that veritable 'tool to end all tools', according to Paul Dirac, the physicist of anti-matter.

Note once again that if the blitz, the 'lightning war' of the Futurists, actually began in the year 40 AD with the geographical invasion of Europe, it was to end, in 1940, with the shutdown delivered by the lightning over Hiroshima, then Nagasaki, thereby indicating, more clearly than a thousand suns, the fission of the critical mass of a terrestrial globe soon to be divided between two antagonistic blocs.

Releasing fossil energy in aid of renewable energies meant, in sum, making the SOLID the enemy in this 'Time War' of an historic acceleration that would end by destroying the city, all the cities, even more surely than strategic air raids. The 'war of the present instant' far outstrips the 'war of movement' that had itself contributed to eliminating the siege war of an era when the solidity of ramparts still protected the city, the railway station contributing, even more surely than artillery, to the disappearance of the fortified enclosure.

In the end, this is where the ultracity looms up, as far back as the nineteenth century, at the same time as the invention of photography and in anticipation of the airport terminal. It does so at the exact moment that Niépce feared 'the loss of value of solids whose contours are fading' but had not yet divined that the persistence of urban sites would end up in turn being blurred in the exurbanization of the resettlement of nations, the forced exile of populations.

We can now better understand the omission, the negation, of the immortality of the soul in postmodern philosophy and the prohibition on hoping for eternal life in the age of a relativity in which Einstein's eternal present would shatter the history of long durations through the illuminism of the speed of light. That new absolute was also to contribute to the decline of the historical materialism of the communists of the Eastern bloc, even more surely than to the decline of the liberalism of the capitalists of the Western bloc!

Surely we can't go on any longer, today, letting ourselves be fooled by the extravagant excesses of a progressive propaganda that is more eco-systemic than truly ecological and that aims at stopping urban sprawl in order to build up city densities around multiple towers that will, they say, be hybrids. … And this, in the remote perspective of some kind of 'sustainable development' for a society once again respectful of 'long durations', a society that will again light up the extinguished theatre of History, even as the great post-urban transhumance of urban agglomerations is being organized, in secret: the future *révolution de l'emport*, the portable revolution, will, in the twenty-first century, put the finishing touches on the revolution in rapid transport that was once responsible for the exodus from the country to the industrial cities; the *static vehicle* of the Very High Building (VHB) will then take over from *dynamic vehicles* deprived of energy at once by the exhaustion of natural resources and the exhaustion of banking resources, with the elevator taking the place of the domestic automobile. The train and that bulk carrier, the jumbo jet will even complete this ecosystem of networks supporting a delocalization that knows absolutely no restraint.

Typically, here's what the deputy mayor of Paris, Denis Baupin, has to say: 'We need first to stop producing inappropriate vehicles. Second tack: abandoning cars in favour of public transport and, lastly, we need to make cities more compact, to increase densities around the city center and public transport corridors.'[4]

The European Commission in Brussels is, moreover, talking of encouraging the circulation, from 2012 on, of 'smart' automobile vehicles that

[4] *La Croix*, 30 July 2008.

47

will allow drivers to communicate between themselves as to the state of traffic, weather conditions, speed limits … and, for 2030, the driverless
car, with the road network infrastructure itself
steering these new station wagons, the distance
between the different vehicles then being controlled by speed sensors which will regulate the
traffic even more surely than hitching railway
wagons together does.

Actually, all of this has now been overtaken by
the issue of energy and especially by the pollution of long distances involved in grey ecology, a
veritable telluric contraction of the terrestrial star
and its geophysical continuum.

Two physicists at Baylor University, what's
more, have just launched a theory according to
which the internal combustion engine could soon
yield its primacy to a *distortion engine* that would
entail bending space-time around the vehicle; the
vehicle would then no longer really move – this
time, its surrounds would.[5]

---

[5] *Sud-Ouest*, 10 August 2008.

We note, then, that in this futurist fable the static vehicle carries the day once and for all over dynamic vehicles (train, plane, ship, rocket …), with the polar inertia of technical progress confirming what Wernher von Braun, for one, prophesied: for want of learning how to drive a vehicle, we will, one day or other, have to learn how to drive the space that surrounds us!

'Paris is small, that's its true greatness,' wrote Jacques Prévert. At the very beginning of the third millennium, the comprehensive rejection of 'urban sprawl' has a significance that is different from the one touted by the advocates of 'sustainable development' and of an architecture said to be 'of high-quality environmental standard' (HQE). What is in play is an actual reversal in metropolitan centrality, with the static vehicle of the very high tower today carrying the day, and from a very great height, over the whole set of dynamic vehicles of domestic automobility, with the axiality that extended the old urban centre making way for a rising axiality. The 'superficial' primacy of the centre over the periphery disappears in aid of an axis now vertical, where the high dominates the low. The primacy of 'upwardness' thereby takes over from the primacy of the formerly privileged city centre, 'downtown', where the horizontal axis of the expanse of land, and ownership of land, once held sway.

The ascendancy of the metropolitics of future settlement at altitude supplants the ascendancy of the geopolitics of a time when Roman boundary work, the *limes*, the national border, stretched out of sight, thanks to the exotic colonization of foreign lands.

European urbanism, American suburbanism, contemporary exurbanism ... In the twenty-first century, what most menaces our societies is disurbanism at altitude – not disurbanism at longitude, as practised by the Russian Futurists of the twentieth century, those adepts of circulation within the Soviet Republics and of the internal passport. That particular revolutionary practice was one Mao Zedong was to revive with the famous *hukow*, the resident's permit responsible for the one hundred million *mingong*. This floating population, endlessly growing, has now washed up, beached, in the railway stations of China, at the foot of the innumerable towers of, say, Shanghai, where seven thousand new towers are scheduled to be up for the next Universal Exhibition.

Actually, such *sustainable development*, the urgency of which is endlessly extolled, takes up the futurist theory of the famous distortion engine whereby space will be bent around a travel vector reduced to inertia. There is one variable, though. This time, it will be a matter of bending back urban space like an umbrella, with 'delusions of hauteur'[6] set to fulfil the delusions of grandeur that fuelled the classical imperium, the emporium at altitude completing the longitudinal expansion of megalopolitan imperialism.

They say the United States, that innovator of the city skyline, is a boundless empire, don't they? An empire stretching out of sight that the recent

[6] Thierry Paquot, *La Folie des hauteurs*. Paris: Bourin, 2008.

economic globalization has looped in on itself, twice round, with Asia now sitting vis-à-vis and face-to-face.

Bending cosmic space around the astronautical vector, bending back urban space and its geopolitics in the upward perpendicularity of human settlement ... something's missing. We need a third and final term to refer to this dynamic exercise in housing humanity. That term is 'unbending' – unbending the topological space of the city, instead of causing that space to bristle with towers, each one higher than the last, based on the model of the orthogon that is the legacy of 'neogothic' style.

Synclinal, anticlinal – in geomorphology, ground and sky couple in the topography of inclined spaces capable of going beyond the customary limits of the regulated spaces of the architectural tradition, where the ground is discredited in favour of the wall and the roof, and inclines and access ramps are always identified with *falling down*, whereas the vertical edifice and the *falling up* it imposes are endlessly glorified ... and have been, ever since the Tower of Babel!

But let's not forget that, since 2001 and the terrorist attack on the World Trade Center, skyscrapers have been provided with building-parachutes and sometimes even with diving-boards capable of being deployed before the big jump, to prevent the stricken from being smashed along the dizzying facades on their way down.

Over the summer of 2008, numerous French travel programmes launched a fashion for *tree houses*. These cabins in the trees similar to children's Wendy-houses suddenly found themselves adapted to the new 'green tourism'; an upward tourism, such as in Pontivy in the Morbihan, where a tent was hung from a branch of a hundred-year-old beech tree standing on the bank of a pond. Similarly, at Dol-de-Bretagne, eighteen wood cabins perched 5 or 13 metres from the ground are accessible by means of rope ladders.

Ecotourism, for a future aerial tourism – no one knows what we're doing *falling upside down* suddenly for an ideal ultracity where the *automotrice à grande vitesse* (AGV) elevator, a lift using a high-speed electric railcar, will replace the weekend car, in a flight to the zenith aimed at a middle class who just can't afford to sign up for the great *space tourism* enjoyed by the well-heeled. The latter are now sending themselves up into the air, on a quest to see, in broad daylight, the nocturnal space of the ultraworld and to perform, weightlessly this time, the seaside leisure activities offered by this *vertical coastline* that revives, exclusively for them, the attractions offered by the beaches of a continental coastline now decidedly too down-to-earth!

Turning the sky into the most beautiful place on Earth: this slogan of aviation company Air France seems to confirm the trend towards a type of agglomeration where exurbanism at altitude will tomorrow extend the utopia of the disurbanism of the 1920s and 1930s, a time when the highway became the *grand boulevard* in the settlement of linear towns and stretched all the way to the confines of the Soviet Union …

Today, though, the prevailing model is no

longer remote automobility but the high and mighty *locomobility* of a public hoist that turns the tower into the perfect equivalent of the old transporter bridge. The classic building block thereby mutates into a sort of great crane, with the static vehicle of the skyscraper of yore suddenly turning into a dynamic vehicle, as in the architect David Fisher's project in Dubai. This is composed of some eighty storeys pivoting around a 'smart' vertical axis that will allow its passenger-inhabitants to change the orientation of their apartments, and with it, the view, the way you change television stations. And it will do this through voice command. Note that such treehouse exoticism, where the vertical axis carries the day over horizontal axiality, also poses the question of *appartenance* – belonging – and not just of the apartment, private or otherwise.

Actually, if 'the soil below-ground has no native country', according to Abel Ferry, the above-ground VHB would seem to have lost such a thing for all time, or in any case to have lost sight of it.

After intensive 'above-ground' agriculture, the culture and art of the vertical street are indeed very much at issue, with this loss of identity that is not so much national as societal, in which *cooped-up high-rise exclusion* rounds off the exclusion of distant urban outskirts, now abandoned. The vertical ultracity puts itself together around transit corridors and very high lifts – something that homeless vagrants forced to keep moving seem to have understood perfectly well, since they are now taking over apartment-block rooftops and balconies, in Cairo and Latin America and else-where, thereby turning their backs on the street and its associated begging to sustainably set up the suburbs at the top of towers!

This is just one more symptom of the heav-enward 'assumption' under way in which the exaggerated promises of the blast-off of humanity have, it would seem, no more limits: Tematis, an agency specializing in the offer of non-standard activities, has for a time been proposing weight-less flights on board a Boeing 727 that takes off from the Kennedy Space Center at Cape

Canaveral, Florida – as well as from Russia. The plane is specially designed as a 'bathtub' for passengers on board to float around in. Duration of the 'bath': seven minutes. Cost of this vertical seaside sport: 2,850 euros, without counting the actual flight, accommodation and meals ...

At the close of the *Trente Glorieuses* – the 'Glorious Thirty' years from 1945 to 1975 – Cioran observed bitterly: 'We are all at the bottom of a hell where every moment is a miracle.'[7] Today, though certain people still claim the Earth is flat, like a 'multi-modal platform', others urge us to make the city more compact for a so-called sustainable development in which architecture will finally meet the High-Quality Environmental standard!

In the nineteenth century, the railways destroyed fortified city enclosures even more surely than any long-range artillery; in the twentieth century,

---

[7] Emil Cioran, *The New Gods*. New York: Quadrangle, 1974, tr. Richard Howard.

air raids razed the cities even more thoroughly than the barbarians. How, then, in the twenty-first century, can we shut our eyes to the fact that this is where the origins of the ultracity lie? The insecurity of the territories of the old geopolitics is part and parcel of this metropolitics, in which climate threats mean that the sky now prevails over the ground, the soil, and even over the exhausted subsoil, to the benefit of a stateless humanity, doomed to the transhumance of 'extremophile' vitality. All this is in the name of globalization of a non-lieu, that no-place where man's ecological footprint will no longer even allow us to guarantee the history of future generations, now that the fabled 'end of history' is being coupled with the end of the geography of a planetary continuum that has become too constricting.

'Have mercy on us who live on the frontiers of limitlessness and the future,' wrote Guillaume Apollinaire. Of course, if, in the face of the endless deluge of accidents and catastrophes of all kinds, we no longer have time to be frightened, we do, on the other hand, have space, all the space of a minuscule planet where acceleration prevails, today, over the accumulation of goods and wealth.

'God's wondrous creation is sometimes experienced as almost hostile to its stewards, even something dangerous,' observed Benedict XVI. Micromega, as Voltaire would say, illustrating the fact that, from now on, the speed of Progress is the old age of a world reduced to property without heritage or donation, whose unnatural dimension does away with all 'sustainable' expanse, since instantaneity and ubiquity eliminate the ancient tripartition: past–present–future.

If we have long lost the depth of time of the past and of long durations, this 'post-historic' wreck actually not only invalidates the future, the depth of field of rising generations. It also invalidates the present, the present tense of an 'event-based history', caught up and then outstripped by a purely 'accidental' history whose tragic imminence no one wants to acknowledge.

Listen, for instance, to Bernard Veyret, a research director at the CNRS who has been tied up studying the effects of electromagnetic waves since 1985: 'I only tell what I know at any given moment. I try to be honest on the day.'

This bizarre declaration is evidence of what has happened to memory and of a nascent futurism of the *real instant* of which the honest scientist becomes one of the prophetic revealers, after that anthropologist of the present, Marc Augé.

'Slow news is no news!' The adage of journalism then becomes the adage of the historian of the instant: 'Slow history is no history.' Far from the fabled 'presentism' of the likes of François Hartog, instantaneism is no longer even the present tense stuck at the intersection of the past and the future, a more or less radiant and progressive future. It is in fact the accident to end all accidents that Aristotle had an apocalyptic premonition of.

So, the accident of real time takes over from the event of the present tense of short durations, in the face of the very long durations of the history dealt with by the Annales School. This explains the impact, right now, on the metropolitan agglomeration, of the sudden acceleration of the real shattering the acceleration of history, classical history, before our very eyes – along with the futurism of an instantaneity without a future that is gearing up to take over, in the twenty-first century, from the futurism of the history of a Progress Daniel Halévy denounced, following the delirious excesses of the Italian and Russian Futurists, to say nothing of those of the atomic scientists involved in a big science without a conscience who were responsible for the Trinity Test at Los Alamos.

In the face of this new historic senility, we are forced to observe that, with this hyperrealist futurism, it is the accident that rules and decides for us!

Hence the obligatory reference to the aleatory nature of meteorology and of the mutation in people's daily life into a sort of waiting room where you wait for the unexpected and where what suddenly turns up always prevails over what is here and now, *hic et nunc*, even more than over what once was, not so long ago, in the modern era. The eternal present of Einsteinian relativism replaces the eternal past of classical historicism in these troubled times, when ecologism has cornered the power to instantly move us all and, in so doing, becomes the ultimate figure of a brand new communism: the Communism of Affects. This synchronization of emotions, of sensations, in real time, allows the setting up, more or less everywhere at once, of the community of emotion, made up of individuals, which will take over from the community of interests, made up of social classes, that the standardization of public opinion in the industrial age failed to make concrete. For the information revolution and associated interactivity have managed to achieve this globalization of shared sensations that is now able to totally eliminate the localization of the political which the city, until very recently, was still the historic symbol of. For the city that is our cultural heritage is now contested, just as the national state was, at the close of the twentieth century, when it came under attack for its separatism. In Europe, the decentralization of

Community powers inaugurates the delocalization, for members, of living space. The bursting
of the real-estate bubble in Japan, at least fifteen
years ago now, and the recent subprime crisis
in the United States underscore the decline in a
megapolitan sedentariness of which Tokyo happened to be was one of the monster capitals.

In fact, if the islands, the 'confetti of the
Empire', were yesterday's legacy of a colonial
past, you can bet that, tomorrow, the same will
go for cities, those insalubrious specks of dust in
a national state outclassed by the interactive feats
of globalized instantaneity whose speed of transmission of data and commands is staggering, the
mad rushes of cybernetics being, in the finish, as
dangerous, though in a different way, as the mad
rushes of massed armoured vehicles.

In this sense, the *disurbanism* of the Russian
Futurists of the very early twentieth century did
indeed show us the way, shunting us onto the
sidelines of historical materialism, where the
linear town started the automobile race towards
the confines of proleterian internationalism. That

race is finishing, today, with the *exurbanism* of the futurists of instantaneity, this meteorological relativism that excludes all geopolitical localization exclusively in favour of a hypercentre that has no tomorrow.

In this perspective of the vanishing point of real space, note that in certain cities in what was East Germany, such as Leipzig, Chemnitz and Halle, constant depopulation now affects major public buildings of historic importance for the future of those cities as a cultural legacy. Things have got so bad that local councils are now offering their premises (rent free) to occupants who are required only to maintain them. And this is happening even as covered parking stations endlessly fill up and railway stations extend their grip. The practical purpose of a railway station, which is the boarding of trains, becomes secondary to subsidiary activities more and more reminiscent of the age-old public square in front of a church or public building or the marketplace of the old town centre, even as 'global arterial thrombosis' has become, according to Wolfgang

Tiefensee, the German Transport Minister, 'a cred-ible hypothesis', due to the interminable convoys of heavy goods vehicles that clog up and obstruct the access roads of the European Community.

'Just-in-time and stockless': the mass distribu-tion of populations doesn't spare the city, then, any more than those abandoned warehouses where the *containerization* of the *emporium* is gearing up to replace the *imperium* of bygone days, when accumulation dominated accelera-tion. The capitalization of the territorial expanses of geopolitics in fact greatly favours the staying power of being-there for nation-states and their identity, whereas it is the being of the trajec-tory and that being's traceability that are now gearing up to carry the day, to the detriment of all localization.

This explains the waning of urban seden-tariness, following the sedentariness of deserti-fied countrysides, even if it is still masked by the metropolarization of so-called 'world cities', the outsourcing of the assets of sovereign wealth funds flagging the predictable decline in the former territorial sovereignty of nations.

By way of confirmation, we might cite the money men of the moment, Warren Buffet and Pete Peterson: 'Seventy per cent of America's debt, or 5,300 billion dollars, is held by foreign investors. The debt keeps growing with the crisis, so we should expect an unprecedented economic disaster.' Such a disaster, which would lead, tomorrow, to inextricable 'peacetime' geo-strategic problems, is already driving China to buy up farmable land in Africa and elsewhere on a massive scale.

Today the Middle Kingdom actually has to feed close to a quarter of the world's population, with only 7 per cent of the world's arable land now, further amputated by industrialization and the urbanization of some 8 million hectares. The property bubble of the rural sector is, then, poised to take over where the urban real-estate bubble left off, having wreaked havoc throughout the world for over ten years already …

After the 'twilight of places' desertified or soon to be flooded all along the great deltas and coastal thresholds, the above-ground property of a sort of neocolonialism seems very much at issue.

In 2008, for instance, South Korea, via Daewoo Logistics, the agricultural subsidiary of the industrial giant, bought up half the arable land of Madagascar, or 1.3 million hectares, thereby outsourcing a Korean geography too cramped to feed its native population. It did so to the great displeasure of the Madagascans, 70 per cent of whom live below the poverty line.

Given the current systemic crisis and having lost confidence in the financial markets, where prices have become too volatile, rich countries are buying themselves *faraway lands*, at low cost, relaunching the old slogan of the colonial empire: here begins elsewhere!

What we're seeing with the crash is the mad rush of sovereign wealth funds on the territorial sovereignty of states. And, since agricultural land prices are low, it's an excellent deal, one that will ensure that tomorrow's supplies are secure.

'With fifty billion, you could buy the Amazon,'

Johan Eliasch, a Swedish-born billionaire who is also an environmental consultant to Gordon Brown (and CEO of the company Head), recently declared, promptly sparking the ire of the Brazilian president. Similarly, on the north of Argentina this time: 'A hectare of land is worth barely more than a hamburger!'[8]

Now, there's a vision of the future of the geo-economic appetite of the well-heeled for you, as well as of the voraciousness of the food power multinationals. By way of conclusion, a word about the 'insecurity of the territory' in Madagascar, that great island now reduced to nothing, or next to nothing, where the people's outcry is growing louder, since the land sold, their native land, is also the fatal land of the cult of the dead.

This ancestral cult is still observed and its memory won't disappear with the spoliation of

[8] S. Kauffmann, 'A vendre pays pauvres', *Le Nouvel Observateur*, 24 December 2008, and 'Pays à vendre', *Le Monde*, 28 February 2009.

land. We might ask this question: *when is there a legal obligation to go up in smoke to clear the terrain?* This must be the ultimate figure of banishment from history, with the cemetery vanishing into thin air, as in the concentration camps ...

In actual fact, we are looking on, powerless, at the great wreck of the land, of all lands, in favour of the sky, of the sky's gaseous state, where waves, clouds and the storms they give rise to stir, meteorological features of a celestial body whose solidity gets blurred in the optical illusion of the speed of light.

3 The Futurism of the Instant

Everything is ruled by lightning.

Heraclitus

In the nineteenth century, Progress meant the *Great Commotion* of the railways. In the twentieth century, still meant more the *Great Speed* of the bullet train and the supersonic jet. In the twenty-first century, it means the *Instantaneity* of the interactive telecommunications of cybernetics. So the anachronistic acceleration of present reality certainly does not spell the end of historicity. More importantly, it does spell the emergence of lying, not by omission any more, but by deterrence of the future as well as of the past.

This involves a sudden loss of memory, every bit as much as of imagination, about the future of a too-cramped telluric planet, cluttered – and rendered insalubrious – not so much by rubbish these days as by the illusions it entertains, its great progressive illusions.

Just-in-time and stockless: the exhaustion of the natural resources of the biosphere is measured now not so much in terms of the quantity of reserves to conserve as in terms of duration, of the time limits allotted to all vitality to come. On the one hand, we have exhaustion of biodiversity and, on the other, exhaustion of the necessary geodiversity of trajectories. But especially and essentially, exhaustion of the chronodiversity of a tripartite history and its projects, the usual chronology of which apparently no longer has currency. Past, present and future contract in the omnipresent instant, just as the expanse of the terrestrial globe does these days in the excessive speed of the constant acceleration of our travels and our telecommunications.

As for the atemporary illusion entertained by the historian of 'presentism' and its brand-new regime of historicity, it has merely put the finishing touches on the presentism of the old regime of an event-based history, which in turn disappears in the acceleration of a now untimely reality that has outpaced the acceleration of the history of the long durations of general historicity.

Actually, after the 'event-based' history of short anecdotal durations that kept historians happy up to the twentieth century, the time – or, more precisely, the lack of time – has come for an 'accidental' history, the history of the 'right' moment, the *kairos* of the real time of immediacy and ubiquity. This now not only dominates the real space of geophysical expanse but also duration – both the long and the short durations of the accident in time, a *hyperrealist* time that now hangs, everywhere you turn, over the geophysical continuum of human activity, the whole array of our activities, now suddenly strictly interactive.

This temporality without any measurable duration – except in terms of milliseconds or nanoseconds – totally subverts the very notion of contemporaneity, in favour of an uncertain term, the atemporeity of the right moment along with the Bachelardian intuition that goes with it.

Here we are, then, way beyond the old wars of memory and the collective civic duty that went with them, for we have reached the threshold of the great chronological deterrence and its particularly pathological chronicles … attracted, it would seem, by a sort of atemporal dromological amnesia which will never be anything more than an alternative version of a terrorist balance – the *balance of the computerized terror* of cybernetic instantaneity that will take over from last century's *balance of atomic terror.*

This spells disorientation in knowledge acquired over the course of millennia regarding the spatial environment and the cycle of the seasons; an *integral accident* in knowledge of history as well as of the usual concrete geography that goes with it, the unity of place and time of a secular historicity…. No doubt this is the fatal novelty of the historic tragedy befalling humanity and a Progress that will no longer be exclusively *technologistical* and extraplanetary, but merely human, 'all too human'. Masochism vis-à-vis an abhorred past that no longer passes

muster is now symmetrically doubled with masochism in relation to a future where, for want of
fear, we will, this time, have space, all the space
of a minuscule planet reduced to nothing, or
as good as, by the progress of our discoveries.
The continuum of the celestial object known as
'Earth' puts an end to our 'progressive' ambi-
tions, the finiteness of the 'real space' of the
terrestrial globe polishing off the ample order
of magnitude of the 'real time' of cybernetic
immediacy.

Let's get back to the new notion of accelerating
reality that ends at the foot of the 'time barrier'.

Immediacy, simultaneity, instantaneity and
ubiquity are all so many attributes of divinity that
each allows us to escape the historic conditions
of humanity.

*What is the nature of the excess reality whose
consenting victims we so often are?* What sort of
hyperrealism are we dealing with here, if not
some eternal return of philosophical undermining
of both temporal and spatial perspectives at

once, a renewed calling into question of the vital importance of depth of field as well as depth of time in the (contemporary) present and all representation? The recent issue of megaloscopic (televisual) ubiquity further confirms that historicity has this optical dimension.

Action, not so long ago, *teleaction* or 'teleoperation' of space probes exploring the universe; today, the perspectivist undermining of immediate actuality is not so much directed at the Quattrocento and its pictorial relief within the real space of perception; it now targets historical relief within the fourth dimension, where the omnipresent instant takes over from the vanishing point. The perspective of real time now wins out over the old perspective of real space that was once so good at conditioning the political life of so-called 'modern' nations, with the quest, a prospective quest, for endless 'progress'.

Faced with the geophysical limits of the finite world, we need to put information in perspective if we are going to understand, at last, that if the Earth has become too small for Progress, it is also too small for short-term profit, as today's economic crash amply demonstrates.

Speaking of which, listen to British economist Robert Skidelsky: 'Only God would be in a position to follow the financial crisis, for only God is fully informed, but he doesn't speculate on the stock exchange!'[1] No more, when it comes to that, than he plays dice!

There in a nutshell lies the whole issue of the information revolution currently taking over from the issue of the industrial exhaustion of stocks of raw material.

The abundance of natural resources goes down the more flows speed up. This will shortly reduce to nothing, or very nearly, the geographical expanse of the common world, just like the limits of the interval of time for political action, with the *nano-chronologies* of the right moment now eating away at long historical periods.

'The man who knows everything is afraid of nothing,' claimed Goebbels, the Nazi regime's

---

[1] *Le Monde*, 11 January 2009.

information minister who was nonetheless frightened of the lack of space in a *Lebensraum* that was the original trigger for lightning conquest of the Old Continent.

We can hardly be surprised, after that, at the recent neocolonial conquest of this 'sixth continent' of a virtual space that replaces the real space of the other five. And we can hardly be surprised at the sovereign wealth funds that everywhere threaten the territorial sovereignty of nations, turning the economic crisis into the beginnings of a new world war. An economic-logistical conflict in which 'ecology' will assume its full ideological place, with the *civil deterrence* of populations whose very survival is threatened taking over from the *military deterrence* of the era of the Cold War between Eastern and Western blocs. So, the balance of atomic terror is yielding to the threat of the *imbalance of the Earth* in the face of major ecological risks whereby the 'hot war' of global warming already melting the polar ice caps will soon take the place of the agony of widespread military conflict …

77

If the world has suddenly become too small for profit due to the acceleration of its objective reality, we must mobilize its resettlement, most urgently, by reversing the primordial priority of the sedentary over the nomadic, thereby industrializing exodus, the deportation that stems from this 'delocalization', with outsourcing turning into a strategic phenomenon.

We now have a better sense of the disastrous importance, for the human environment, of this information bomb that disintegrates all natural magnitudes, the very scale of all common reality, whether geographic, cultural, historical, just as the atomic bomb, in its day, was able to disintegrate the 'nature' of the components of matter.

To produce travellers as an anonymous mass and not just *travel* any more, as in the past with the transport revolution – that is, indeed, the dire project of a portable revolution, a *révolution de l'emport*, that is currently starting off with 'global' mobilization in a time of civil peace succeeding the 'general' mobilizations in a time of openly declared war, which the new terrorism has now dispersed.

To mobilize bodies – the social body as a whole – as they have already mobilized minds, the attention of whole populations, through the arsenal of the teletechnologies of the mobile and its multiple screens: this is indeed the unavowed reason for the endless growth in the carrying capacity, the *capacité d'emport*, of the small as well as big vehicles that clutter up the logistical platforms (ports, airports, railways) – *multimodal platforms* – of interconnected networks that will destroy the town, the city and its historic centre, even more surely than the urban highway did last century. The externalization – outsourcing – under way, since the development of the very latest of 'globalizations', looks a lot like yesterday's extermination: the logistical culmination of a massive deportation of peoples at the heart of the foreclosed space of that 'Fortress Europe' of sinister memory.

Whether the expanded time of 'futurism' or the contracted space of 'progressivism', speed, in the twentieth century, proved to be nothing more than the propaganda of a growing disaster.

Whether Italian Futurists or Russian Futurists, fans of the lightning war all the fascisms promoted, all proved to be mere dupes of the self-styled futurism of the instant, right up to this very recent 'enhanced reality' of a virtual space that is a surrogate for the real space of the terrestrial globe.

But let's go back for a moment to the perspective of real time offered by ubiquity, of which Google Earth is just one aspect among others, to this very particular relief that affects not only our subjective and interpersonal relationships, but further, and especially, our connection to the world.

With habituation to multiple screens, the focus of the visual field diverts us from peripheral vision, from the open field that gave its everyday fullness to the real space of the verges of our activities and, as a result, causes disorientation in being-there. The teleobjective proximity of transmission tools thereby considerably alters our grasp of the surrounding environment in which each of us physically evolves.

From that moment, the natural relief of the perspective of real space, a product of the binocular nature of vision, takes on the 'reality effect' of screens. This induces a second type of stereoscopic relief in which the habitual 'objectivity' of our eyes and the instrumental teleobjectivity of cameras suddenly work together to achieve for our sight what the bass notes and trebles of stereophony already induced for our hearing. The 'realism' of observation with the naked eye suffers the impact of the *stereorealism* of this telereality that is never anything more than an excess reality brought on by our eyes' cupidity.

So, with this new relief, the very latest perspectivism of televisual instantaneity, the aesthetics of disappearance finds itself complete: 'See all, hear all, and forget all', as Napoleon directed.

The key term here is indeed that megaloscopic *all* of an excess reality in which totalitarianism is no longer merely strategic and political, but turns into a totalitarianism of a sudden scopic urge that tends to swamp the subject's awareness, in the name of progress in information, with stereoreality from then on blurring the contours of the visual field. Let's not forget journalism's recent adage, here: 'Slow news is no news.'

Contemplation or addiction? This effect of a field between direct perception, *de visu* and *in situ*, and another kind of perception, at a distance and instantaneous; this large-scale relief that is at once stereoscopic and stereophonic, due to the perspective of real-time transmission-reception, is going to totally overturn the conditions of visibility of the existence of each and every one of us, as well as the greater or lesser viability of being-there, here and now, that defines our place in the human group as well as in the world around us where our activities take place.

This is the prospect for hearing and vision and, soon, the paradoxical prospect for touch and tactility at a distance, along the lines of the exotic model already provided by the teleoperations of space probes. What remains, afterwards, of the physical proximity Napoleon also talked about when he observed that 'in love as in war, to conclude, you need to make contact'?

What kind of proxemics are we dealing with in this perspective of instantaneous action as well as of simultaneous perception? Of this *uninhabitable futurism* that claims, once and for all, to supplant the futurism of a history *to come*, but also the *déjà vu* history of short-event durations themselves outstripped, to the sole advantage of the accident of present Time? Or of this 'near future of the instant waiting to be dealt with, on the point of becoming the immediate past' that Jankélévitch spoke about in relation to the collapse of the infinitesimal thread of time for a human being who suddenly becomes the 'angel of the instant'?[2]

Addiction to, or compulsive dependence on, the internet and its innumerable search engines is actually an initial response at the origin of this reality effect whereby interactivity is already

---

[2] Vladimir Jankélévitch, *Le Sérieux de l'Intention*. Paris: Flammarion, 1983.

driving certain of the faithful to quit their concrete environment, to vacate the premises of an organic social vitality, and even to abandon any regular eating, all healthy living, for this full-screen virtual perspective in which the individual, literally consumed by his screens, puts his mental health in danger through habituation to the hallucinations induced by a pseudo-relief that wins out over the full-scale dimension of all physical reality.

In the end, this is what it comes down to – this 'acceleration of reality' that now not only conditions the history of a new and pitiless century, but the instant, every past instant. And does so in favour of an instant not so much present as omnipresent, in a diminished world that is not so much 'contemporary' with some banal history of modernity as *atemporary.* In that world, the Earth, already too small for Progress and for short-term profit, all of a sudden becomes too cramped for our future projects, *the expansion of the instant wiping out the beginning every bit as much as the end,* the geophysical finiteness of the life-giving star. You may well have your life before you, but the world, the world before you, the biosphere as unique *objectum* – what's that?

In the end, this is what it comes down to – this globalitarianism that they're always going on about in relation to some 'single market' where, thanks to progressive habituation, the megaloscopy involved in ubiquity leads to excess lying by deterrence of the past and of the future, as of all objective reality. What is promoted instead is a virtual illusion that will take over, they say, from the life-size dimension of an 'ecoscopic' planet Earth, that will be reduced to nothing, or as good as, to a tiny little insalubrious object in the sky that will come under the political ecology of threatened nations.

That world will not be *before you* much longer, carried as it is by the stroboscopic illusion of accelerating real time and its progressive tyranny. Very soon it will be *behind you*, behind your back, thanks to the exoticism of a miserable extremophile life, whose privileged means will be exobiology, with its genetic bomb, the third of its kind.

Recently, you could read this sentence by an author who shall remain nameless: 'The ultimate promise is within our grasp: that nothing happen any more anywhere, ever – unless we say so and man finally reveals the god within.'

With this declaration of principle, less revelatory of the futurism of the instant than 'revelationary' of the ambient madness, totalitarian engineering unveils its programme, pulling down the Wall of Chance, after the Berlin Wall and then Wall Street. This is in anticipation of the supreme software of some 'Great Computer' destined to produce the World of the Great Object in the sky, ecological terraformation on the part of a geo-engineering that has located its training ground here below, before later going on to colonize the exoplanets of the solar system.

So, the demi-angelism of the angel of the instant, heralded by the philosopher of the almost nothing, will be succeeded by the sun worship of ubiquity and of simultaneity for a transhistorical illuminism prefigured in the *cosmism* that flourished in the last days of the Soviet Union and is reproduced in today's *cosmotheism*, in the name of a revived *Lebensraum* – or, more precisely, a *Lebenszeit* that will thumb its nose at chance in the name of the ecosystemic necessity of the procedures involved in a cybernetic salvation whereby Edgar Allan Poe's *Angel of the Odd* will take on post-human features, for a New Age that will finally have come to pass!

Note that in Canada, in any case, the think tank, Global Footprint Network, declared on 25 September, 2008, 'Earth Overshoot Day' since, between January and September 2008, humanity consumed all the resources it takes nature a year to produce.

This mournful calendar, designed to give already anxious souls a jolt, was in fact drawn up by the people who came up with the concept of an ecological footprint in the first place, in the wake of the Earth Summit of 1992, where William Rees and Mathis Wackernagel finessed measurement of the impact of mankind's activities on our ecosystems by quantifying the Earth's biologically productive surfaces. Global Footprint

Network in turn allows us to quantify the evolution of consumption of natural resources over time ... the time that remains, obviously, before its *mise-en-abyme*.

We note, then, one more time: since planet Earth has, it would seem, become too small for Progress, and, in a word, insalubrious, we are so pressed on all sides that we not only no longer have time to feel fear, we don't even have a future for our plans. ... All that then remains is space, all the tragi-comic space of an expanding universe accelerating towards the Big Crunch, the end of time as well as of cosmological history!

So, this is it, this dromosphere of eccentric acceleration that dominates the history of our pathetically feeble powers (political, economic), reopening, with the magnitude of power of Progress, the issue of the very nature of a world now foreclosed and of this biosphere that, as certain astrophysicists already suspect, is the only one of its kind.

With this absurd notion of a time without a future or a past worthy of the name, the ecology of the human chronotope turns into an ecology of what's lacking, of the scarcity of resources that are not only substantial but *distantial* – in terms of duration, of the time that was once present and is now disqualified by the very brevity of the 'accident in knowledge' of which the stock market crash remains the most true-to-life caricature.

On that subject, the quarrel of contemporary historians over the retrospective criminalization of history is nothing more than a panic-induced consequence of the taboo that today targets the future, the future of the whole panoply of our progressive aspirations.

We could even add that the active secularization of history mentioned earlier, which tends to build up mono-atheism as a sort of stereoscopic double of monotheism, is merely the pursuit, by other means, of this *prohibition on imagining any form of transcendence*, perspectival or prospective, physical or metaphysical. The nihilism of the suicidal State, inaugurated in the twentieth century, continues to wreak havoc beyond the balance of terror of mutually assured destruction, beyond the successive fall of the three Walls …

Indeed, if the historian has lost his role as 'lay prophet' of the 'time war', he has been replaced by the journalist, the archivist and the man of the mass media and soon, even, if we're not careful, by the legislator, the judge of the unthinkable!

Once the 'public prosecutor of the past', as Michelet hoped, such a judge, Pierre Nora specifies, will have changed tense: 'Today we'd like the historian to play the role of public prosecutor of the present.'[3] Unfortunately, as we've seen above, the present doesn't now pass muster any more than the past, driven as it is to disappear *ex abrupto* in the right moment of a repeat accident, for a historicity that will soon be as automatic as the gearboxes of our latest vehicles, a superior form of *media coup* that will tend, this time, to shut down the theatre of history once and for all in aid of its *cinéma d'actualité*, relaying current affairs.

[3] *Le Nouvel Observateur*, 9 October 2008.

90

Concerned about the retrospective moralization of history and intellectual censure, we call for the mobilization of European historians and for the wisdom of politicians. History must not be a slave to contemporary politics ... In a free state, no political authority has the right to define historical truth and to restrain the freedom of the historian with the threat of penal sanctions.

That is the opening of the 2008 Blois Appeal, a demand for 'the freedom of the historian' that saw a thousand or so historians rallying behind René Rémond and Pierre Nora, calling into question not only History with a capital 'H', but the contemporary historicity of the information revolution.

A revolution in instantaneous information that is overturning the chronotope of our daily lives to the unseen advantage, it would seem, of a chronotype of accelerating historic time in which the instant dominates all duration from now on. This explains the characteristic assault on memory and *memory activism* which is in the end nothing less than the triggering – economic and political – of the first War of Time for a world in the grip of its own accelerated spatiotemporal finalization.

This is indeed one of the unacknowledged aspects of the globalization of a real time that subverts not only the real space of the geography of the globe, but also our relationship to time that is really *present*, since we know from experience: 'It's always questioning the present that causes us to question the past.'[4]

Speed and politics of the regime of historicity. … The information revolution and its time bomb are merely the austere revelation of the finiteness of the pace of history and its tripartite chronology.

Which explains the sudden acceleration of common reality these days and the 'excess reality' that subverts our past history – but also the contemporary history of a present rendered inert and inconsequential in the face of the chronotype

[4] Jean-Pierre Rioux, *Le Nouvel Observateur*, 9 October 2008.

of an instantaneity that causes us to escape the geo-historic chronotope of everyday activity.

Surely we can't fail to sense, if not actually understand, that the crash of the year 2007, which continues relentlessly to this day, is in no way analogous to the crash of 1929, but rather to that of 1987. That crash closely followed the setting-up of programme trading, that is, the instantaneous interconnection of stock exchanges that the Anglo-Saxons, what's more, were to call the Big Bang …

Memory loss? Widespread amnesia? What? Leaving out the Asian crash of 1997 and the blowing up in full flight of the Internet Bubble, surely we can hardly deny, today, the 'excess reality' of the models, the mathematical and digital programmes, that not only shape the audiovisual landscape of current affairs, but also the space-time of a single market in which the Brownian Model of aleatory processes carefully overlooks the excessiveness of an objective risk and only takes into account the teleobjective risk run by the cameras of a market now once and for all global. In that market, the statistical mean always wins out over the untimely accident, the breaks in continuity of present history. The frantic automation of stocks and securities management on the stock exchange takes practically no account of the accidental nature of a historicity whose pace is no longer calibrated, as it once was, by the event of outstanding importance.

On that score, this is what Nicole El Karoui, head of the Master's Course in 'Probability and Finance' at the Université Pierre et Marie Curie, has to say: 'We need to create warning systems before we set up new rules. We need to create a barometer of financial activities that can warn us about overheating.'[5]

Global warming on the one hand, economic overheating on the other: honestly, disaster anticipation is becoming so widespread we'll soon need to set up meteopolitics in place of a geopolitics that is obviously too 'down-to-earth' now that atemporal futurism is gearing up to swamp

[5] *Le Monde*, 2 October 2008.

the secular shores of general history before too long!

'I started with nothing but, so far, I've lost nothing, either,' Mike Davis remarked sardonically as the members of the G7 gathered in Washington to try and dodge the 'systemic shock' of the American crash – even though that system, the whole point of which is to engender chaos and the repetition of serial crises, could well lead before long to the economic war of each against all, a third world war of a new kind.

Indeed, we now urgently need to review the very nature of a system that above all sets panic among all. To change, if not the turbo-capitalism of the single market, then at least the software it uses.

We need to abandon this fatal logicism that has for so long overlooked the psychological side of our behaviours, of our objective rationality, and instead driven us into a definitive loss of confidence, not only in the past of our beliefs (philosophical, religious, and so on), but also in our everyday lives – if we don't want to

95

shortly end up despairing of a future that has no future.

One question keeps coming back today: can the political economy of the wealth of nations remain much longer in automatic mode as it has been since the crash of 1987 – the famous Big Bang of the markets at the end of the 1980s which led us directly to the Big Crunch of credit and of traders' confidence that we are currently going through?

Listen to the experts: 'Whereas banks record the market price for each of their stocks according to the international financial reporting standards (IFR), what we'd need to do is to swap these stocks with *the historical acquisition prices*, which would mean nothing less than a return to traditional accounting, abandoned most imprudently five years ago already.'[6]

For his part, Immanuel Wallerstein, a sociologist and disciple of Fernand Braudel, declared in the autumn of 2008:

---

[6] Marc de Scitivaux, 'Plan Paulson: les raisons d'un retard à l'allumage', *Le Journal du dimanche*, 12 October 2008.

Capitalism isn't managing to hold together as a system any more in the sense that physicist and chemist Ilya Prigogine understood. When a biological, chemical or social system deviates too much and especially too often from its stable state and doesn't manage to get back into equilibrium, we see it split in two. The situation then becomes chaotic, uncontrollable for the forces that controlled it till then.[7]

Being metastable, open systems always renew themselves. The closed system, the foreclosed system, on the other hand, collapses in on itself and implodes. This is what is happening today with the world economy. The magnitude of power then gives way to the magnitude of poverty.

If the Earth has become too small for Progress, it is also too small for reckless short-term profit and, in that sense, Immanuel Wallerstein is right

---

[7] 'Le capitalisme touche à sa fin', *Le Monde*, 12 October 2008.

to predict that 'capitalism is nearing its end and the possibilities the system offers for real accumulation have reached their limits.' But Wallerstein, it would seem, reverses the movement under way, for it is the end, finiteness, which is nearing the turbo-capitalism of the single market.

The end of quantities and stocks of all kinds is now hitting head-on a world economy stretched to the limit, between the flows produced by endless acceleration and the all-time low of available stocks that always enhanced the lure of money for the powerful, just as the geographical scale of the continents attracted the colonial conquerors.

'For what doth it profit a man if he gain the whole world, if he loses or ruins himself?' In other words, if he loses his soul, his *anima*, in the inertia of an acquired world. And that is indeed what is happening with a *single market* where everything is now played out in the real instant of globalization, where the excessive speed of just-in-time delivery of profit dominates the excessive wealth of the vanished stocks of a *world economy*, so dear to Braudel, which will soon have to make way for the *world ecology* of restrictions of a new order …

Still according to Braudel, though cleverly taken up by certain economists: 'Ever since the thirteenth century, capitalism would act a bit like an internal combustion engine which would be improved every time there was trouble, from one crisis to the next.' Maybe. But if the twentieth century innovated the reaction engine, or jet engine, the twenty-first, it would seem, is gearing up to invent the art of an implosion engine; the black hole, so ardently searched for by our physicists in quest of missing energy, perfectly symbolizing the reversal involved in an unnatural project that would allow us, at last, to differentiate between matter and anti-matter!

Strangely, these days, no one judges it necessary to reconsider our relationship to time. More to the point, no one is analysing the consequences of *the improbable long term* of a 'progress in energy' in which the duration of the harmful effects of nuclear power, for instance, can be counted in hundreds, if not thousands, of years. Similarly, a big song and dance is made about the great saving in calculating time the computer allows. In physics and biology, for instance, with the decoding of the human genome, thousands of hours put in by experienced researchers have been replaced by hyperactive software programs not dissimilar to those used by traders for tracking profits, with the toxic risks we are all only too familiar with. Nanometer, nanosecond, even picosecond... The nanotechnologies pose the fatal question of nanochronologies.

Past, present, future: once more, what remains of the long durations of history or the short durations of the event in the face of the lack of duration involved in instantaneity, if not the beginnings of an accidental history and a purely anecdotal historicity?

Whether we are dealing with the infinitely big of historicity or the infinitely small of instantaneity, the question forced on us, today, then, concerns the history of the accident in time and in classical temporality; not just the history of the temporality involved in the 'astronomical' durations of the damage done by Progress, but, especially, the history of the lack of duration of our diverse activities and, beyond that, of the interactivity of human relations soon to be synchronized.

For want of an improbable end of history, this would have to be a sign of the imminent extinction, not of the human race, but certainly of the chronodiversity of sentient life. A panic-inducing phenomenon that the Futurists of last century longed to see. Here's Marinetti, for one, in 1913:

Man has acquired one by one a sense of his home, a sense of the neighbourhood where he lives, a sense of his geographical region, and finally of the continent. Today he is aware of the whole world. He doesn't need to know what his ancestors did, he needs to know what all his contemporaries all over the world are doing. ... He must feel himself to be at once axis, judge and motor of the explored and unexplored infinite. Hence his urgent need

101

to establish relations with all mankind at every instant.[8]

So, the 'Great War' is no longer just 'the world's only hygiene' any more, as Marinetti announced it was in 1915. It is already the hygiene of Time, a time that comes along to the detriment of a past that we are supposed to forget; a war of time more than of world space. The blitzkrieg of *escape velocity* will prove to be that war's propaganda, on behalf of an extraterrestrial and exobiological liberation whose outrageous absurdity – the hubris of a historicity without true duration – was to be flagged by the conquest of space in 'the balance of atomic terror' between Eastern and Western blocs.

---

[8] Marinetti, 'Imagination without Strings and Words-in-Freedom', quoted by Maurizio Serra, *Marinetti et la révolution futuriste*, Paris: L'Herne, 2008.

Index